PARK BOOKS

A Flower for the Dead Friedrich Achleitner

The Memorials of Bogdan Bogdanović

PARK BOOKS

Photos
Friedrich Achleitner
Illustrations
Bogdan Bogdanović
© Architekturzentrum Wien
Translation
Jonathan Quinn

Book Design and Production
lenz+ büro für visuelle gestaltung
gabriele lenz und elena henrich
www.gabrielelenz.at
Typefaces
Sabon, Jan Tschichold, 1966
Imago, Günter Gerhard Lange, 1982
Paper
Surbalin glatt, 6185 Kaffeebraun
Arctic Volume 150 g/m², 170 g/m²
Printed by
Ueberreuter Print GmbH

© 2013 Park Books, Zurich

Park Books
Niederdorfstrasse 54
8001 Zurich
Switzerland
www.park-books.com

Published by agreement with Paul Zsolnay Verlag Wien, Vienna
All rights reserved

Printed in Austria
ISBN 978-3-906027-35-7

The publication of this book was made possible
by the generous support of

Contents

6	Foreword
8	Location Map
10	**Belgrade** Memorial to the Jewish Victims of Fascism
16	**Sremska Mitrovica** Memorial Cenotaph to the Victims of Fascism
24	**Mostar** Partisan Necropolis
40	**Jasenovac** Memorial to the Victims of the Concentration Camp
58	**Kruševac** Slobodište Park, Symbolic Necropolis with Open-Air Theatre
68	**Kosovska Mitrovica** Shrine Dedicated to the Serb and Albanian Partisans
80	**Prilep** Cenotaphs to the Fallen Soldiers of the Resistance
86	**Leskovac** Memorial to the Revolution
92	**Knjaževac** Memorial to the Fallen in the Wars of Liberation, 1804–1945
100	**Štip** War Grave
110	**Bihać** Cenotaphs in Garavice Memorial Park
122	**Čačak** Memorial Site with Mausoleum for 4650 Fallen Partisans
132	**Bela Crkva** Group of Cenotaphs
138	**Travnik** Cenotaphs for the Victims of Fascism
144	**Berane** Monument to Freedom
154	**Vlasotince** Shrine to the Fallen Freedom Fighters
162	**Vukovar** Dudik Memorial Park for the Victims of Fascism
170	**Popina near Trstenik** Combatants' Mausoleum
180	Afterword and Acknowledgements
183	Bibliography

Foreword

The vocabulary of contemporary architecture theory is incapable, or hardly capable, of describing the memorial sites of the urbanist, architect, sculptor and essayist Bogdan Bogdanović. This Serbian-born European was not only the architect of around 20 memorial sites spread throughout the territories of former Yugoslavia he was also an unorthodox urbanist, a card-carrying Surrealist, so to speak, and a lateral thinker. He was a writer of calibre, too, and a politically declared anti-nationalist who was driven out of the country by Milošević, subsequently spending the last years of his life — from 1993 to 2010 — in exile in Vienna.

Today his supranational, multiethnic, transreligious and life-affirming memorials are among the most impressive artistically conceived commemorative sites inscribed into the European cultural landscape. They are also places that provide impetus for a new co-existence for people from different ethnic backgrounds and regions, of different nationalities and religions. These memorials, commemorative sites, mausoleums and necropolises are places that — even though often beleaguered by monsters set in stone — take a positive approach to life and the future while also pointing beyond their time. It is no coincidence that many of these sites are popular among young people and families with children who play there. While most recent memorials impair reflection or even hinder it B.B.'s memorials encourage, even inspire, reflection. They do so without preaching or prophesy, they do not communicate any certainties either, they are in no way didactic, neither counting nor recounting, and they do not settle any scores but lend their full weight to content, allowing as much room as possible for the events being commemorated. Usually made with the most enduring materials and the utmost craftsmanship and artistry, the memorials focus attention on their subject matter.

Not only do these works by B.B. hold a special position in the context of European modernism they are also clearly recognisable one-offs in the entire history of the culture of memorials in twentieth century Europe. They repudiate the narrative representation of heroic deeds or crimes, avoiding the illustrative and avoiding emotively charged allusions to historical events. They take on neither the tasks of historical documentation nor of historical research and mediation. This would be commemoration on a different level, one that remains the remit of the museums and archives. The monuments do not make a show of the crimes' perpetrators or help to attract attention, albeit negative, to them. Instead they are places that affirm continuing life and give the nameless victims, and those named too, a place of commemoration, a place to be remembered by.

Although the work of B.B. would be inconceivable without its modern roots (for instance, in Surrealism) it did not subscribe to the zeitgeist, to the doctrines of the everyday politics of the time, to a linear belief in progress or even to the imagery of political ideologies. Exceptionally well-educated, and knowledgeable even about prehistoric times, Bogdan Bogdanović was very capable of producing inventive work that was informed by European and non-European cultures without becoming historicist or even eclectic. His commemorative objects are freely invented, with symbolic allusions that defy definitive interpretation. B.B. had an aversion to purely rational, narrow-minded explanations of the symbolism, he embraced its inspirational energy (even heightened to the level of the fantastic) while still being playfully open to its interpretive and deeper implications.

Today the memorial sites form an interrelated cultural network stretching beyond the borders of the republics formerly constituting Yugoslavia, and they have become symbols of ancient relationships and conflicts: The cultural diversity of Jasenovac and Vukovar, Popina or Prilep, Čačak, Mostar, Bihać, Berane or Kosovska Mitrovica symbolises the uniting commonalities, and the separating differences can only be understood with first-hand experience of the respective landscapes and local cultural contexts. Bogdanović's approach is inclusive rather than exclusive, cohesive rather than divisive. He has left a legacy for the countryside and the people he loved here that they presumably cannot yet grasp, a legacy that is inscribed indelibly into their cultures; this legacy is a promise for the future. He did everything he could have done, he was not able to do more but he did do that, to paraphrase Bogdanović.

This book is not an architecture history essay nor is it a study based on art- or culture-historical research, and it is by no means an attempt to delve deep into the archaic depths of B.B.'s world of allegorical and symbolic imagery, nor to interpret it. This report is, as a view from outside, the result of a friendship with Bogdan and Ksenija Bogdanović that lasted over ten years, and of many conversations and several trips to all of the memorial sites. The long and intense engagement with his work and, not least, my promise on the day before his death to write this book give me the courage to do so. It can only make a small contribution to studies and analyses to come: for I am certain that this incredibly diverse body of work will invite research by future generations of experts on architecture, art and culture.

Friedrich Achleitner

Location Map

1. **Belgrade** Memorial to the Jewish Victims of Fascism
2. **Sremska Mitrovica** Memorial Cenotaph to the Victims of Fascism
3. **Mostar** Partisan Necropolis
4. **Jasenovac** Memorial to the Victims of the Concentration Camp
5. **Kruševac** Slobodište Park, Symbolic Necropolis with Open-Air Theatre
6. **Kosovska Mitrovica** Shrine Dedicated to the Serb and Albanian Partisans
7. **Prilep** Cenotaphs to the Fallen Soldiers of the Resistance
8. **Leskovac** Memorial to the Revolution
9. **Knjaževac** Memorial to the Fallen in the Wars of Liberation, 1804–1945
10. **Štip** War Grave
11. **Bihać** Cenotaphs in Garavice Memorial Park
12. **Čačak** Memorial Site with Mausoleum for 4650 Fallen Partisans
13. **Bela Crkva** Group of Cenotaphs
14. **Travnik** Cenotaphs for the Victims of Fascism
15. **Berane** Monument to Freedom
16. **Vlasotince** Shrine to the Fallen Freedom Fighters
17. **Vukovar** Dudik Memorial Park for the Victims of Fascism
18. **Popina near Trstenik** Combatants' Mausoleum

Belgrade
Serbia

Memorial to the Jewish Victims of Fascism

1951–52

The memorial is inserted in an existing Sephardic cemetery, on the axis of a small alley that continues as a path enclosed and paved as a dromos by two low walls. This leads to a pair of powerful 'wings' of stone with a V-shaped passage open to the sky: a portal, a threshold? The wings are actually wing-shaped in an elevating gesture, like open arms.

1

A seven-branched symbol appears (like a menorah) in the middle of the portal that used to stand amid the open view down to the Danube, i.e. that opened up an unobstructed view into a deep tract of the Danube floodplains. Large trees occupy the background today so that this termination casts the view back onto the memorial itself, or at least delineates it as a ward within a district.

The young Bogdan Bogdanović originally wanted to cast the 10.5 metre wings in concrete, the method of the time. However the Jewish community insisted on natural stone. Hence the stone cladding of a concrete core and a change from the walls' having a structural impact to having a surface impact emphasised by a kind of setting for the edges (like a decorative border). With this the young architect discovered the tactile impact and the sensual impact of stone. This seems important to note because it is an early signal for the subsequent rejection of a tectonic, structural line of thought for a textural, ornamental one.

The accompanying low, stone walls were indeed laid in a kind of collage technique, with different stones and a large number of glyphs that signify concrete memories for the community. They stem from destroyed Jewish homes in the historic district of Dorćol. For the contemporary visitor they are a bizarre sign of a collective memory, a wall newspaper of history carved in stone. It is also interesting that the Jewish community insisted on having the ensemble signed on a small plaque (which was not done at subsequent memorials) as if the architect ought to receive recognition while also adopting a kind of subjective responsibility.

2–4

The fact that at the beginning of the 1950s and still under Stalin the monument entirely opts out of the conventions of socialist realism is shown by plump searches for the ideological symbols of the time. The same questions, repeatedly: Where is the red star? Where are the hammer and sickle? This first commemorative site by the architect thus already displays, as do many elements of his later works, the emphasis on a path accentuated, for instance, by sculptural and spatial elements, or the particular significance of spatial sequences: the temporal element in the spatial experience. Initially single-minded, stringent, self-confident, so to speak, until it reaches irritations and finally arrives at an ambiguous resolution. As if an astonished cluelessness and a sanctified confusion remain as the only possible responses in the face of our ultimate destiny.

It must be taken into consideration, and Bogdanović later developed a kind of principle from this, that in the political situation immediately following the war it was impossible to use clearly unambiguous symbolis without becoming involved with the official political symbolism — which had always been trivial in semantic terms. In this regard, the philosophy-trained, humanist-educated and surrealistically baptised 'Luchs'(German for lynx, a nickname that B.B. enjoyed into old age) B.B. found a way out of the dilemma of ideological symbols.

The urn containing Bogdan Bogdanović's ashes was laid to rest close to the rear left gate on 28 September 2010.

1 2 3 4

12

Memorial to the Jewish Victims of Fascism

Belgrade, Serbia

14
Memorial to the Jewish Victims of Fascism
Belgrade, Serbia

Sremska Mitrovica
Serbia

Memorial Cenotaph to the Victims of Fascism

1959–60

The complex runs along the existing Serbian Orthodox cemetery (on the site of the murder of civilians during the Second World War by the German occupying forces and the Croatian Ustaše) and blends unbordered into the neighbouring municipal park, which calls to mind an English-style landscaped garden. The memorial is organised along an axis and links (over a stretch of more than half a kilometre) two symbolic elements, a six metre tall copper amphora (or urn) and a square surrounded by eight pyramid-shaped grave mounds symbolising the six former republics and two autonomous provinces of Yugoslavia, which are themselves crowned by leaf-shaped, copper flame sculptures. The connecting axis (and ultimately the square) is bordered on both sides by knee-high, carefully structured little walls made of exposed protruding brickwork that accentuate the dromos without disturbing the view of the landscape. The amphora is split into two so that the visitor standing upright sees the slit at their own height and is invited to enter the impressive, even enigmatic and contemplative space. The split hollow provides the loosely structured countryside with a point of focus and reflection. It is entirely in keeping with the architect's intention: this setting can be appreciated in very different ways, for instance as a place to play for children and youths or as a place of reflection by older people.

One could describe the site as more archaic in comparison to later such projects because the elements here (axis, path, earthen pyramids, sculptures, monumental features etc.) accord with entirely familiar commemorative elements.

Apart from its existence in the urban recreational space's being taken for granted today, the complex also reminds the visitor of the way symbols change over the course of history: once symbolic of the state of Yugoslavia through the presence of the constituent republics, they now allude to the co-existence of different states in a shared space that is re-aligning itself politically and can look forward to a better future.

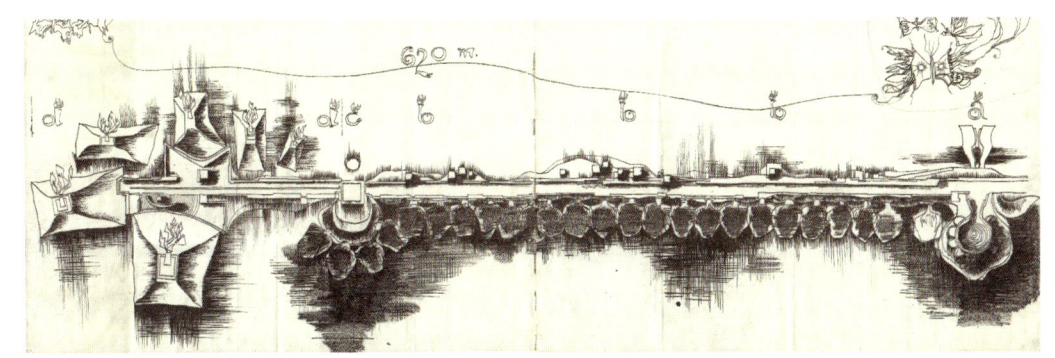

17

A Flower for the Dead

1   2   3   4   5   6

18

Memorial Cenotaph to the Victims of Fascism

Sremska Mitrovica, Serbia

20

Memorial Cenotaph to the Victims of Fascism

Sremska Mitrovica, Serbia

22

Memorial Cenotaph to the Victims of Fascism

Sremska Mitrovica, Serbia

23

Mostar
Bosnia and Herzegovina

Partisan Necropolis

1959 – 65

Assistant architects: Dimitije Mladenović, Sima Miljković, Vlada Veličković

The memorial is a necropolis laid out on seven terraces, and one of the commemorative masterpieces of the twentieth century, deliberated on and conceived in a context of many epochs of cultural memorialisation without becoming lost in historical features or even in historicity. Associations are allowed with landscape architecture, archaic and antique cult sites, baroque belvederes, or garden concepts from different cultures. The terraces with the small, individually designed and inscribed commemorative plaques lying on the ground lend collective commemoration an individual, almost familiar character.

The design (see plan) presents a thoroughly interesting concept. The necropolis unfolds along three axes of about 250 metres in length on the side of the Biskupova Glavica hill that stretch towards the highest point at an angle of about thirty degrees to one another. The first immediately appreciable axis forms the guiding line for the meandering path up to the cemetery. This leads, from the Kralja Petra Krešimira IV road across a large forecourt with paving reminiscent of the floor plan to a baroque roadside chapel, through a lion's gate to (currently dry) water steps, which are accompanied by two paths with parapet-like stone walls. Having united, a single paved path winds its way across a grassy hill and along a high wall (called the cemetery wall) to the entrances. This upward route is also enclosed by high walls reminiscent of the accessways to medieval castles, and leads to the terraces, which themselves open up the view of the city of the living in steps as a staggered vantage point.

The channelled supporting walls with cosmic symbols (the sun, constellations of stars etc.) define the open-air setting of the acro-necropolis, they run in waves along the topography, accentuating it sculpturally. A unique setting, certainly, but free of heroic pathos: The effort invested in the quality of the planning, the artistry, the craftsmanship and the materials alone show the respect due to the dead.

That is the view of the space that the path upwards offers. Once on the uppermost terrace a radical change of direction is conveyed with a kind of bird's-eye view. An overview opens up along a second axis that makes an arena-like space of the cemetery with a strictly geometric arrangement, whereby the round pond situated close to the entrance shifts onto the axis. The result is a baroque garden concept that can compete with any historical ensemble. The layout of the ascending path with the varied and striking spatial experiences subjects itself to a higher order of dialogue between nature and architecture. The third axis marked on the plan cannot actually be seen in the realisation, it clearly establishes a relationship with the plan of the city that is not visually manifested in the construction.

1

2

3

4

5

6

A necropolis for 810 members of the communist resistance who fell in the conflict with the Croatian Ustaše and the German occupying forces.

I was somewhat reserved regarding this construction, which was presented in the print media as formally overloaded and overburdened with ornamentation. The reality shows entirely different interrelationships, however: the ornaments and symbols only mark points, they focus attention on particular spots. The heavy texture of the walls, their reliefs and the channelling are sucked-up by the distance, by the vegetation, by the light, by the patina etc. (which B.B. valued highly); as a whole, certainly a *theatrum* (Ristić) but one that retains emphasis on the atmosphere of an architectural space embedded in the natural setting in the foreground. The innumerable lovingly designed little details remain modest elements of a concerted overall concept.

6, 12

The stringent concept behind the play on movement of the walls, the enclosed sites, is revealed at the summit. The main axis of the terraced space structured by the fountain and the circular pond, the forecourt and the gate, water steps and path are visible for what they are, freestanding elements in the topography, a staging of the ascent that only becomes part of the larger plan from the height of the cemetery. While walking up, the apparently straight course of the water steps makes the round pond look like a solitary element outside the complex, in reality it is situated on the main axis, it is the visual backbone of the impressive view of the city, the metaphor for the unity of life and death, a dialogue between the architect and urbanist Bogdan Bogdanović and the city. To express this in a paradox: Bogdanović is a master of 'precise suggestion', the synthesis of collective memory and its expression in the oldest media known to the plastic arts.

10

The ensemble is now in a deplorable state following the devastation during the Balkan Wars. However traces of careful restoration and reconstruction are to be seen. And the litter discarded by visitors is the smallest of the challenges to be faced. The fountain, the water steps and the pond used to be fed by a pool situated in the forest that has fallen into disrepair.

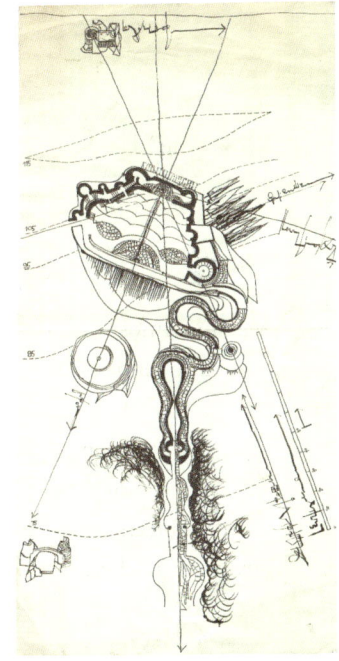

7

8

9

10

11

12

13

26

Partisan Necropolis

Mostar, Bosnia and Herzegovina

28
Partisan Necropolis
Mostar, Bosnia and Herzegovina

30
Partisan Necropolis
Mostar, Bosnia and Herzegovina

Partisan Necropolis

Mostar, Bosnia and Herzegovina

34

Partisan Necropolis

Mostar, Bosnia and Herzegovina

36

Partisan Necropolis

Mostar, Bosnia and Herzegovina

38

Partisan Necropolis

Mostar, Bosnia and Herzegovina

Jasenovac
Croatia

Memorial to the Victims of the Concentration Camp

1959–66

Of course, entering the Jasenovac memorial site on a glorious autumn day with a blue sky and white cotton-wool clouds one asks oneself what this placated beauty, this metaphorically transformed landscape with the sky-scraping, almost thirty metre tall concrete flower, what all of this has to do with the horrors of a concentration camp. After leaving the modest museum with the classical atrium and the framed view of the marshy plain complete with the enigmatic symbols and a small wood, and leaving behind the bullet-hole strewn village, the visitor moves on to an embankment flanked on one side by an abandoned railway line alongside the river Save, concealed behind floodplain forestation so out of sight. This river marks the border with Bosnia. The floodplain landscape is captivating; the 'concrete flower' standing in it fits the proportions of the natural setting transformed into an artefact.

A goods train stands at the end of the tracks with cattle waggons and an old steam locomotive, the only real allusion to the horrific events of the past. This fragment of the memory looks like a gesture of respect for a subject, and even more so for the victims themselves, deserving of decidedly more realism, more illustration, more eye-witness reporting and a recognisable allocation of culpability even in the planning and the construction. More than that, it says: commemoration is an act of continued reckoning in a place of Never Forgetting. But no reckoning begins in Jasenovac, no tally of any kind is kept. This installation with the train for the transport of the victims is a later addition by a different architect.

The railway tracks continue as a path made of old sleepers and lead onto a gentle hill from where there is an overview of the floodplains, and to the actual memorial, which lies behind a brickyard pond (visitors are on the site of a former brickworks). A local sculptor has put a bronze table on the hill bearing a plan of the site. It provides welcome information on the composition of the concentration camp that once stood there, which was itself obliterated having fulfilled its own remit of extermination, and has left almost no traces. The positions of the barracks, the workshops and other buildings are marked on the damp ground by domed tumuli, calling to mind grave mounds sunk into the earth but also mutated marsh bubbles rising as eerie messages from the ground of history.

The Subject Matter

Of the eighteen major commemorative sites created by Bogdan Bogdanović throughout Yugoslavia over around four decades, Jasenovac was the fourth. The planning began back in 1959. So one could say Jasenovac belongs to the earliest memorials, and the search at that time for the appropriate architectural means is not without the dramaticism of inner

1

2

3

4

5

An Ustaše death camp where Serbs, Jews, Romani and anti-fascists of many nationalities were murdered in unknown numbers.

positioning. In B.B.'s autobiography, *Der verdammte Baumeister* [The doomed architect], there is an extensive passage on the decision-making process, the course of the planning and the realisation. The reader cannot avoid this testimonial, and in it lies the key to all of the commemorative sites. I quote a number of sentences:

The beginning: In the course of my work on the planning of the monument in Jasenovac it was frequently suggested and even expected that I preoccupy myself with the photographs, the records, the paperwork and eye-witness reports from the few surviving inmates of the camp. I avoided doing so, pushed it to one side, and two or three times I explicitly declined to engage with the material. The sadistic details were stifling, they made me breathless and ruined my concentration. I apologised and tried to explain that I was quite capable of understanding and feeling the metaphysics of the crime, which was also true. The agonizing documentation just depressed me and confused me, and ultimately only meant more work. I knew, by the way, that I would neither look for nor find inspiration by bringing the evil back to life.

You have to picture the political situation in Yugoslavia during the early 1960s: socialist realism in the Stalin era might have been overcome but anti-fascist monuments intended to remind people of extermination camps, partisans etc. were inconceivable without the emblematic red star, the hammer and sickle, and fighting, dying and victorious figures. In addition, Jasenovac was a special place, and all trace of the camp had not been eradicated for no reason.

Jasenovac was probably the last place of execution in Europe that had nothing left to remind people of its past… On the other hand, there was a reluctance to clearly express and provide evidence of what Jasenovac had actually been. The infantile attempts to add this concentration camp to the list of Hitler's crimes (the formulation crimes committed by the occupying forces and their collaborators *was very popular) were not particularly clever as Croatia had not been occupied. So such formulaic approaches met with opposition, not only from Serbs and Jews but also from German anti-fascists. The latter alluded to the extent of German guilt, they did not need another country's disgrace added to that…*

Strange as it might appear: The Gestapo had condemned the camp regime because Hitler prescribed an 'impersonal' form of mass-murder. A crime committed with a personal emotional investment was considered psychologically and politically very risky… They were reluctant to begin erecting a monument because its completion would have amounted to an admission that it had been a Croatian extermination camp…

A Flower for the Dead

6

7

8

9

10

11

12

One must remember here that Bogdan Bogdanović came from a surrealist tradition as an artist, he was also familiar with an extended psychological temporal horizon. If shapes were at all capable of leading a way out of the intricacies involved with the allocation of guilt — the perpetuation of the crime and the mutual allocation of accountability — then these were images from an archaic form of remembrance and the overcoming of hate through the utopia of mutual understanding. The stance taken by Josip Broz Tito in deciding on the construction of the monument signalised this sense of helplessness in the face of the almost insoluble problematic issues involved. And perhaps Bogdan Bogdanović found the right words at the right moment when presenting his project, which was met with little sympathy from the comrades.

At the end of my presentation, however, without changing my tone of voice and in order to explain the spiritual aura of the proposed monument, I resorted to a few long words such as, for example, 'aesthetic metaphysics' or 'the interdenominational ritual of the setting' or 'anthropological, general human memory' and so on…

He [Tito] had even understood my warning that it was not possible to talk about issues of good and evil, of crime and punishment, of life and death on the level of Marxist chrestomathy [useful learning]…

The extremely sensitive decision making process on a political level behind the Jasenovac monument is described by Heike Karge with great precision in her essay 'Von Helden und Opfern' [On heroes and victims]. The question was: *Why did Tito and his political allies settle on this undertaking in 1960? Where and how this challenging location had been treated until then — a place where it was not heroic combatants who had to be commemorated but murdered Serbs, Jews, Romani, Croats and others, a place that simply did not conform to the official ideal of 'Brotherhood and Unity' and the associated pathos.* Money was only to be spent on monuments that stood for the sublime and the great. But public pressure grew so strong that they decided to erect a monument.

Karge: *We know that Bogdan Bogdanović's flower was deeply upsetting to the political leadership. For in contrast to all of the earlier ideas and project proposals that had been designed for Jasenovac, only Bogdanović understood how to erect a monument worthy of the victims of this challenging place of remembrance.* Tito never visited the site.

The role of symbolism is actually the core theme in the work of Bogdan Bogdanović. In this, too, he distanced himself most from the rationalist, functionalist or constructivist tendencies of the twentieth century. Curiously enough, as at least in its roots Surrealism had

Memorial to the Victims of the Concentration Camp

Jasenovac, Croatia

shown a scientific interest in psychological processes and attempted to lay footholds of rationality in the mires of the subconscious. But Bogdanović:

I never deliberately looked for symbols. As strange as it may sound, they found me. They overcame me and led me to unexpected thought processes and discoveries. For the monument at Jasenovac the structural concept — I am tempted to say the allegory of the statics — spontaneously fitted the visible syntax of the formal vocabulary, and I was very proud of that.

In the chapter 'Der Raub der Symbole' [The theft of symbols] in *Der verdammte Baumeister* there is also a clear statement describing his fascination with and distance from the subject of symbols:

I have always been suspicious of the experts who trust themselves to interpret the symbols explicitly with lexicographic precision. Sometimes I felt a silent rage when I read that this or that idea, which was usually taken entirely out of its original context, was supposed to mean precisely this or that and nothing else. Such manifestations are pointless because one cannot pinpoint the essence of the symbolism… the symbolic imagery heralds from another reality for mankind that one can only penetrate intuitively and with the aid of the miracle of personal imagination… Put more simply, I avoided forcing my own notion of an otherworldly order onto other people. On the contrary, I enjoyed eavesdropping on other people's interpretations, even those concerning my own work.

The Concentration Camp – History and Museum

Jasenovac was an extermination camp run by the Ustaše on the grounds of an old brickworks where Yugoslavian anti-fascists of all political persuasions were killed — along with Jews, Romani and other minority groups. The total number of victims is entirely unknown (estimates vary between 80,000 and 800,000). There are few traces left because, as is historically documented, most of the victims were thrown into the bordering Save river. Practically nothing remains of the camp buildings. The Croats originally rejected the erection of the memorial site because it had been designed by a Serb; it had been rejected anyway by the Serbs because it was not clear to them what was being commemorated here, what the historical events had been. Following the disintegration of Yugoslavia and after the last war Tuđman wanted to turn Jasenovac into, in his own words, 'a national Pantheon' where the Croatian heroes' gallery (with himself included) was to be assembled. He did not succeed. In the meantime Bogdan Bogdanović has become a highly renowned persona grata in Croatia because of his stance against the Milošević regime and especially due to his decidedly

anti-nationalist position. The memorial site is supplemented by a small museum attractively positioned in the landscape that is run in exemplary fashion by a young director (Nataša Jovičić) and being extended as a collection. The museum is a key element in the thematic complex of the memorial. It assumes the task of providing objective information so it is not required of the artistic means of expression, which (see socialist realism) could never have accomplished the task.

The Design Process

Along with the plans, there are hundreds of hand-drawn sketches that clearly show how deeply B.B. delved into the subject matter and developed the design. One should not imagine that this development was linear, he encircled the topic continually. Of course there are a number of thematic foci, such as the engagement with the landscape, the formal manifestations of the interventions, the connection with water, the vegetation, the search for artistic elements, whether one dominant monument — a flower or blossom — or several small ones. In the concentration on one large all-dominating structure the issue of its positioning arose, the connection with the ground, the boundary to the site (trench, parapet, wall, plinth etc.). Should the substructure be developed spatially, for instance with a crypt, what should the transition from the ground to the stalk and to the crest look like? The blossom alone represented an inexhaustible subject. Innumerable studies were made of petals, as well as attempts at the flower/blossom/crest, until eventually a structural spatial and gestural unity was achieved that lends this construction, this sculpture, its fascination today — and which Bogdanović himself described as static allegory.

In the execution of the extremely complicated casting process and far removed from today's measuring and computer technology Bogdan Bogdanović was lucky enough to find an excellent Montenegrin engineer, retired at the time, who was capable of realising the bold, freestyle lines of the sculpture with the aid of some Dalmatian shipbuilders. The documentation and an analysis of the construction process would be extremely interesting. As Yugoslavian architects were also trained in statics and as structural engineers, Bogdanović was (so he said) able to do the calculations himself.

The Village, The Memorial, The Landscape

Jasenovac is small village with a population of a few hundred. The traces of the last war are still visible, houses have been partially destroyed and abandoned. The small museum lies at the edge of the village, flat buildings with an atrium between them (designed by Petar Vovk,

Memorial to the Victims of the Concentration Camp
Jasenovac, Croatia

1

2

3

4

5

1   1968, interior design: Leonida Kovač, permanent exhibition: Helena Njirić). From the atrium there is a (framed) view of the memorial site. The museum forms the basis for all of the information down to the smallest details. Here, too, it is not about facts and figures, there is nothing didactic in the approach nor is it in any way tendentious. This means that visitors to the memorial are informed about the location, about what happened, the past, when they enter the site.

The memorial itself is a transformed landscape, a visionary artefact. A metaphor with-
3   out anything concretely metaphorical. But what is a metaphor then in this context? Certainly not that a concrete meaning should be ascribed to this ensemble of elements in the landscape, to the path to the monument and its not being straight, leading over an artificial hill
5, 6   and running between two small ponds. Bogdanović loved plays on meaning, suggestion, and left room to think the contrary. Mounds of earth blend into the gentle play of the water and grass surfaces, reed-covered banks and clusters of trees. Some of these mounds are half-sunken into a round hollow, some rising from flat ground like grave mounds. The tumuli, which initially only mark the positions where buildings once stood, workshops and the camp barracks, draw the visitor's imagination towards the burial places, but a curious relationship arises to the ground lying beneath the water that has engulfed so much history and from where these monstrous bubbles emerge. The apparently idyllic location turns into a metaphor for transience and return and exudes a threatened calm. Floodplain landscapes have a relationship of their own to time, they are waiting for the unforeseeable. The nature seems to react more indifferently, elastic, more adaptably. In contrast, the human interventions
3   battle with the *fury of disappearance*.

Many visitors take the direct path to the monument and do not leave it, or become lost in the layout of the grounds, which is even reminiscent of a thematically interlinked Land Art installation. I delayed approaching the 'flower' for a long time, I had the impression of
8 – 12   a violent explosion petrified in concrete shooting out of the ground like a geyser. The view on coming closer slowly transforms the vast sculpture into a flower, the plays of light and shadow become more lovely, more accepting. The theme of growing out of the ground, which the architect engaged with in innumerable sketches, appears to have been surprisingly simply
7   resolved despite the imaginativeness of the gesture. The base, which conceals an additional space reminiscent of a crypt, presses to the surface like a root stock, and the 'blossom' rising above it looks liberated and buoyant. The brittle reinforced concrete that it is made of

6

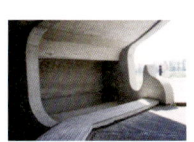
7

8

9

10

11

12

develops a musical lightness. The term 'musical' is not inappropriate as alongside its spatial turbulence the biomorphic shape also develops turbulence acoustically, it is a sound chamber, an instrument that not only communicates spatially with the breadth of the plains but also with the sound of its winds, even with the twittering of the birds.

The Jasenovac memorial is above all a place of remembrance. It is impossible to wander through this place and leave it untouched. And all of the symbols and metaphors that one thought one had seen are ultimately condensed into one of the simplest of human gestures towards somebody who has died: lying or placing a flower on their grave. Bogdan Bogdanović has placed a massive flower into the landscape for those who found death in Jasenovac, one which is also a sign of remembrance that everybody can understand.

47

48

Memorial to the Victims of the Concentration Camp

Jasenovac, Croatia

50

Memorial to the Victims of the Concentration Camp

Jasenovac, Croatia

52
Memorial to the Victims of the Concentration Camp
Jasenovac, Croatia

54

Memorial to the Victims of the Concentration Camp

Jasenovac, Croatia

56

Memorial to the Victims of the Concentration Camp

Jasenovac, Croatia

Kruševac
Serbia

Slobodište Park, Symbolic Necropolis with Open-Air Theatre

1960–65

First impression: a modern landscaped park, sculptures, small dense clusters of trees; a semi-circular reception building placed into the ground with a small round forecourt, and with an owl made by Bogdanović as a sentry. The building is a kind of small culture and information centre. Is it also by Bogdanović? No. By his former student Svetislav Živić, in the late 1970s. Access via an earthen wall with a round stone gate, today half-open at the top, in front of which is a round lawn with a tree. Between two mounds of earth, moving on through a ditch to a broad, gentle, kettle-like open space bordered by woodland (The Valley of Remembrance). Is this where people were shot? Yes. No. Yes. This used to be a flat field. During the course of work the complex was transformed into an artificial, inviting, also playful landscape. The gigantic earthworks were made by a local bulldozer manufacturer who used the site to test their products. On the ground is a millstone with an inscription in Bogdanovićian lettering, rough translation: *When you stand beneath this sky, stand upright.* Twelve enigmatic, approximately three metre long stones lie in the hollow, shaped like Minoan horns, others claim to see butterflies, that wander — or flutter — up to the woodland in a loosely curved row (in two groups of six stones each), their ends bearing grimacing faces. Are they gruesome creatures, monsters, used innocently by children and youths as objects for playing on, lying on and climbing? A strange location. Where is the open-air theatre? We go back, turning away from the ditch up a hill, and see an antique theatre in a second, somewhat more geometrically lain hollow, The Valley of the Living. Overgrown. Only the suggestion left of the stands, an archaeological memory but usable. A space in-waiting that also permits any other use to be made of it. On the other side, right on the edge of the woodland, stands a light cross on a stringently structured surface. Here lie about 600 victims. Being a commemorative spot they keep their distance while nevertheless still being present, but not right in the middle of the town's recreational or leisure park. At the entrance Stockholm's south cemetery came spontaneously to mind, Skogskyrkogården. Gunnar Asplund, the great Swedish architect, was also capable of transforming landscape into art, into poetry. Here the play with the ambivalence of thought and perception is even more radical. Bogdan Bogdanović ties death to life, it is as if he wanted to remind people that the one could not exist without the other. His memorials do not monumentalise death, they do not add pathos to the cruelty or to irreconcilability, they are the opposite: when all of the monsters of this surreal world have once again been vanquished they even permit the occasional snigger. Bogdanović calls the commemorative landscape of Kruševac

1

600 anti-fascists and hostages were executed on this spot by the German occupying forces and Serb collaborators.

a *symbolic necropolis with open-air theatre.* The theatre as a symbol for the continued life of generations to come.

Second visit: We visit the memorial, remonstrated by two older Serbs because the Germans committed far more appalling war crimes, then they are arrogantly judgemental about acts of cruelty committed by Serbs. Young people are in the complex again, mothers, too, with children playing. A second visit highlights the normality of the place. A harmonic balance prevails between the landscaped natural setting and the artefacts.

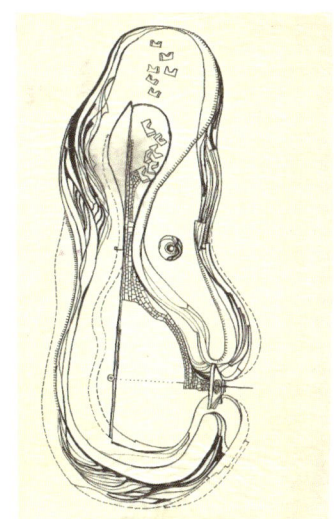

2　　　　　3　　　　　4　　　　　5　　　　　6　　　　　7　　　　　8

60

Slobodište Park,

Symbolic Necropolis with Open-Air Theatre

Kruševac, Serbia

62
Slobodište Park,
Symbolic Necropolis with Open-Air Theatre
Kruševac, Serbia

64

Slobodište Park,

Symbolic Necropolis with Open-Air Theatre

Kruševac, Serbia

66
Slobodište Park,
Symbolic Necropolis with Open-Air Theatre
Kruševac, Serbia

Kosovska Mitrovica
Kosovo

Shrine Dedicated to the Serb and Albanian Partisans

1960–73

Assistant architect: Dimitrije Mladenović

Statics: Božidar Boža Petrović

While many of the memorials by Bogdan Bogdanović form places for thinking and remembrance either in an urban situation or in open countryside, the cult site of Kosovska Mitrovica is first and foremost a symbol in the urban fabric and the surrounding countryside clearly visible from a distance. As a symbol not only on a mountain (Mali Zvecan) but also on the ethnic border between Albanian and Serb settlements, it is initially an open door that does not lock or even exclude but, open on both sides as a symbol of connection, commemorates that both ethnic groups fought German fascism together and died for the same cause. Historical events have hardly changed this symbol but they have transformed its meaning. It can be read today as a peaceful call for generations to come to bury the old conflicts and to encounter each other with understanding at least. The symbol succinctly says no more and no less than that the doorway produces an open connection from the north to the south and from the south to the north.

The gate structure is, though, more than a calligraphically striking symbolic landmark. The powerful, strongly tapered and almost twenty metre tall columns (with grainy concrete surfacing), reminiscent of the ancient Doric style, support a huge reinforced concrete trough that used to be clad with copper and, in the coal-mining community it was then more than today, called to mind a rail-bound coal carriage called a 'Pitdog'. Today, following the closure of the pits, this symbol is now only a reminder of Kosovska Mitrovica's past, and sad proof of how quickly the message conveyed by a monument can change. The architecture historian Ivan Ristić interprets the two columns as a symbol of the brotherhood of both Kosovo populations, which does not lessen the connection between both columns with what they carry. There is also another clearly legible aspect to them: The two massive columns, conical concrete tubes cast on location (approximate lower diameter: five to six metres) only leave a small passageway open while the doorway is wide open at the top. It could be presumed from this that the reality (the passageway) is different from idealized allusions to the historical connection between both ethnic groups. One thing is certain: the monument has a dual significance. On the one hand as a real and an impressive door in situ, on the other as a symbolic landmark dominating the city and the countryside. Such visual presence has only been achieved by a few monuments in the world. The calligrapher Bogdan Bogdanović was aware of the power of symbols that were capable of inscribing themselves on the view of a city and the surrounding countryside. The entrance originally planned for the site of the shrine was to have been from the city (on the river) but it was not realised for reasons of cost.

1

2

A Flower for the Dead

3

4

5

6

7

8

9

Shrine Dedicated to the Serb and Albanian Partisans
Kosovska Mitrovica, Kosovo

72

Shrine Dedicated to the Serb and Albanian Partisans

Kosovska Mitrovica, Kosovo

74
Shrine Dedicated to the Serb and Albanian Partisans
Kosovska Mitrovica, Kosovo

76
Shrine Dedicated to the Serb and Albanian Partisans
Kosovska Mitrovica, Kosovo

78

Shrine Dedicated to the Serb and Albanian Partisans

Kosovska Mitrovica, Kosovo

Prilep
Macedonia

Cenotaphs to the Fallen Soldiers of the Resistance

1961

The city lies amid a fascinating landscape, a broad vista bordered by a picturesque range of mountains. However, embedded in a mundane world of recreation, the cenotaphs lie on a park-like plateau that blends into a gentle forested incline down to the city. According to Ivan Ristić, Tumulus of the Unconquered, as it is known, has largely been realised (with a 115 metre long axis) without any reference to the appropriate plans, which can be also be seen from a sketch of the site plan by B.B. Knowing this, one also suspects that the geometry of the existing complex has been simplified (for instance, ovals to circles, the omission of flowing forms etc.) to make the implementation easier. Nevertheless, there is a fascinating concept behind the axial relationship between the cultic dance floor and the uncovered

3, 4   circular space (and being an inverted conical section it is also reminiscent of archaic calendar structures) inserted in the grave mounds, with plaques engraved with the names of the fallen

2   Partisans. The seven dancing figures are particularly impressive, they are approximately three metres tall and accordingly heavy Janus-faced white marble figures in the shape of inverted Ionic capitals that take the weight from the figures like hats, almost making them hover. Here, as is so often the case in B.B.'s work, the introverted space of death is contrasted with a natural setting where life flourishes. It is a metaphorical stage-management, though, that reaches back into the depths of human history. The seven female figures are accompanied by another approximately four metre tall figure (a lead male dancer) whose role is open to interpretation by visitors but which probably alludes to local dance rituals.

Approaching the cenotaph from higher up the view is initially of the tumulus with an axially arranged stone staircase; taking the latter provides a fantastic view over the complex and down to the city. At the same time one could find the small stalls (between

2   the figures) on the dance floor selling souvenirs to tourists irritating, but this is a part of life in places of pilgrimage and commemorative sites.

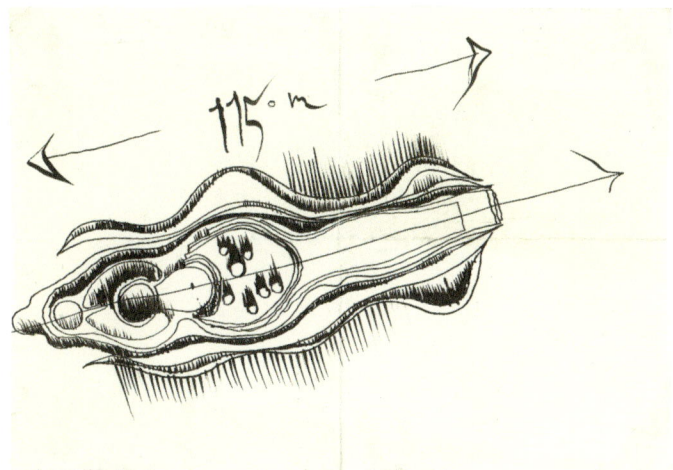

81

A Flower for the Dead

1   2   3   4

82

Cenotaphs to the Fallen Soldiers of the Resistance

Prilep, Macedonia

84

Cenotaphs to the Fallen Soldiers of the Resistance

Prilep, Macedonia

Leskovac
Serbia

Memorial to the Revolution

1964 – 71

Assistant architect: Dimitrije Mladenović

The memorial develops along a sloping site that is accompanied by a road higher up.
1   A wooden doorway as a frame marks the entrance to the complex, then a stone path (half a kilometre long) at the foot of the slope leads along to the actual memorial. A circular arena
2   with flat steps (about twenty metres in diameter) is occupied by an excentrically positioned,
3   twelve metre tall, stone-clad amphora (recognisable as a female figure). In the inner ring there are eight 2.2 metre high prismatic stelae with floral ornamentation in relief, and another ring with thirty 1.2 metre tall stones in groups of two, four and six. Here, too, a free but still organised grouping of the elements, the groups are arranged intimately, calling to mind Bogomil graves or Turkish cemeteries.

    A little girl once associated the massive, majestic-looking forest goddess wearing
3   a curious headpiece — the earrings have disappeared — with Liz Taylor, much to Bogdan Bogdanović's delight. As a whole, cryptic and multifaceted symbolism but a very atmospheric location, where when we visited it (at midday) an old man with a pram was passing the time. To be found as well in the adjacent forest is a row of staggered, approximately fifty centimetre tall prismatic stones that have no direct relationship to the memorial cemetery except for a stone path. According to a statement by Prof. Mldanović, Leskovac is the first complex where B.B. worked with arrangements of grouped prismatic stones in the space.

A Flower for the Dead

1　　　　　　　2　　　　　　　3　　　　　　　4

88

Memorial to the Revolution

Leskovac, Serbia

90
Memorial to the Revolution
Leskovac, Serbia

Knjaževac
Serbia

Memorial to the Fallen in the Wars of Liberation, 1804–1945

1969–71

6

3, 4

1, 2

5

A 'city within a city', a city of the dead as a living monument. The floor plan of a Roman encampment in the town centre, with a main axis (from the town gate to the river Timok) and an intersecting route with an agora as an open arcade of wood that is, on the other hand, slightly reminiscent of Chinese garden architecture and actually only covers a bench, enclosing a relatively large square area where people of all ages pass the time alone or in groups. A place taken for granted, where it is easy to relax and exchange gossip. Here, too, commemoration is deliberately connected with everyday life and the immediate life of the town.

Commemorative stones (like gravestones in a cemetery) in various sizes and in groups (each symbolising one war) mark separate areas. The connection to the river with a small bridge permits associations with memories of Josef Plečnik's riverbank development in Ljubljana. The urbanist Bogdanović has succeeded in generating urbanity with little effort because he had the capacity to think in long periods of time and understood the town as the cradle of all cultures.

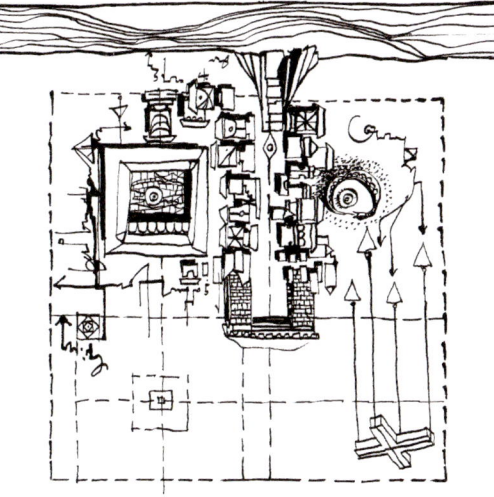

93

A Flower for the Dead

1   2   3   4   5   6

94

Memorial to the Fallen

in the Wars of Liberation, 1804–1945

Knjaževac, Serbia

96
Memorial to the Fallen
in the Wars of Liberation, 1804–1945
Knjaževac, Serbia

98

Memorial to the Fallen
in the Wars of Liberation, 1804–1945
Knjaževac, Serbia

Štip
Macedonia

War Grave

1969–74

The complex, lying beneath the ruins of Isar Fortress, consists of two terraces and three archaic elements: the tripartite portal, the split double staircase (on the lower terrace) and the terrace with twelve 2.2 metre tall stelae. The doorway consists of three freestanding parts without a cover piece and is primarily the architectural emphasis of a threshold, a valuable symbol for the separation of two mutually exclusive areas. The steps, however, consist of a narrow, gentle ascent on the right, fitted to the site with pedestal-like landings (changing direction with the terrain), and a single flight that is straight, direct, steep, monumental and enclosed by stone slabs engraved with the names of the fallen. Thinking about Bogdanović's fine craftsmanship, these plaques seem somewhat mechanically or factory-made.

The twelve gravestones on the second terrace stand in the long, slightly curved row and are visible in the distance from the valley and from the town. The white marble looks like new. The boulders with the large rosettes (or suns) and similar symbols look a little like mouldings at first glance, even decorative. The fine, subtle detail as well as the surface ornamentation of inimitable ingenuity on the sides can only be appreciated on closer scrutiny. Here, instead of the usual stonemason's technique, the expression is permitted to be in the hew of the stone.

1

2

3

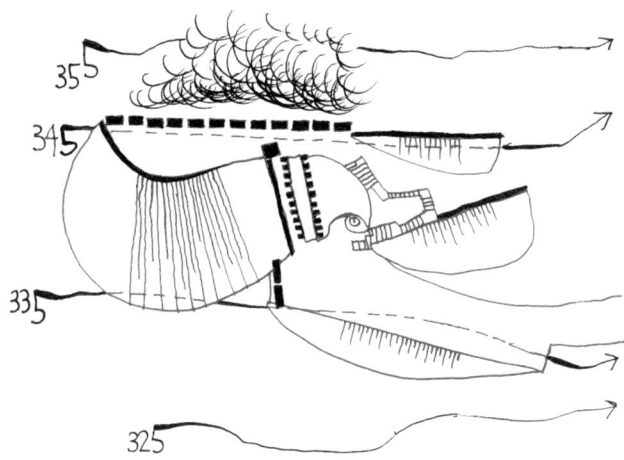

A Flower for the Dead

   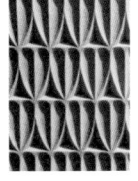   

4   5   6   7   8   9   10

102
War Grave
Štip, Macedonia

104
War Grave
Štip, Macedonia

106
War Grave
Štip, Macedonia

108
War Grave
Štip, Macedonia

Bihać
Bosnia and Herzegovina

Cenotaphs in Garavice Memorial Park

1969 – 81

Assistant architect: Dimitrije Mladenović

Statics: Bozidar Boza Petrović

Garavice Memorial Park is one of the most impressive destinations on a journey to the works of Bogdan Bogdanović. The former execution place (for mass shootings by the Croatian Ustaše), one of the hills dominating the bucolic landscape, is occupied by eleven 'Mourning Women', as they are called, (anthropomorphous megaliths) spread over the mountain in loose groups. B.B. is a master in the organisation of constellations of freestanding elements in context. One is led almost magically through each web of interrelationships and drawn into the spatial dialogue between the figures. The landscape is open, undeveloped, an extraordinary natural setting not yet worked over nor overworked by farming and through which herds of sheep still pass today.

Each of the upright figures made from four stone blocks (standing on a stone base edged with steel bands) has a construction that approximates the human figure. There is a leg zone, a lower body and a torso part, and finally the head; each zone is marked differently. On the uppermost blocks of stone (heads, or faces) traces of a human mimesis of mourning can be discerned, for example in tear-like engravings. At the foot of the hill the wailing figures stand farther apart, lonely, becoming denser towards the top to form a compact group in collective mourning.

Characteristic for Bogdanović's work are the routes that the paths take into the constellations of elements used. The hill is initially approached along a lane with shrubs on both sides, past a small paved surface (a square) and then ascending the hill in broad curves. The network of paths becomes tighter, the spatial interrelationships of the figures less relaxed, until finally the group condenses into a solid manifestation at the summit. This is the innermost area, where one discovers that the figures are not talking to one another but each for themselves, facing outwards, declaring their mourning to the visitors.

On the way back it is as if one were following a network of small brooks uniting in a stream that feeds into a pond which forms the starting point for visitors as a small, round, paved terrace.

Note: Ivan Ristić drew my attention to later chiselling on the figures by an untrained hand that does not really cut into the stone, perhaps these are the commentaries of a subsequent generation. Bogdan Bogdanović apparently responded positively to these interventions, which would be entirely in keeping with his approach. One could also say that the power of the figures does not lie in the detail but in the cubic construction, in their huge presence on the hill and in the landscape.

1 2 3

There are two figures similar to the ones standing in mourning on the hill to be discovered on the east side of the road coming from the north (shortly before the entrance to the memorial site). A riddle yet to be solved.

4

5

6

7

8

9

10

112

Cenotaphs in Garavice Memorial Park

Bihać, Bosnia and Herzegovina

114

Cenotaphs in Garavice Memorial Park

Bihać, Bosnia and Herzegovina

116
Cenotaphs in Garavice Memorial Park
Bihać, Bosnia and Herzegovina

Cenotaphs in Garavice Memorial Park
Bihać, Bosnia and Herzegovina

120
Cenotaphs in Garavice Memorial Park
Bihać, Bosnia and Herzegovina

Čačak
Serbia

Memorial Site with Mausoleum for 4650 Fallen Partisans

1970–80

The agricultural land forming a kind of aisle (like a flat slalom slope) through the forested sides of Jelica mountain is occupied in the upper zone by three objects standing in a line, the contents of which initially remain unclear. Are these agricultural buildings? Their pitched roofs suggest barns or hay racks. The hurried visitor drives past an open-air staircase situated in the shadow of the forest at the foot of the hill, and ends up to the side half-way from the top at a providently planned car park. In the middle of the lower end of the slope lies an approximately one-storey high, rather well trodden grave mound which opens the view upwards. This view is of four monoliths (Herzegovinian gabbro) arranged to comprise a freestanding stone doorway with two openings to the three objects that slowly reveal themselves when approached, together with the reliefs of the stone pillars standing side-by-side, as a temple. This ensemble is, obviously for topographical reasons, slightly off-axis so there is space on the left side for an opening with a pipe to channel off occasional excess water from the slope. Only now is the composition balanced and the abstract configuration of the complex bound to the location.

The view from the grave mound again opens into an impressive sequence of spaces, this time only between two points, the archaic gateway and the temples with their Gloriette-like hilltop vantage-point position. The extremely well emphasised perpendicular axis cannot be appreciated from below, and it almost erases the memory of that initial view. The temples are transformed into three doors standing one behind the other, the gaps in-between are slits where the fall of light is aggressive. The ground is paved as a path and ends on both sides with different height stone steps in pedestal-like landings that lead into the terrain (the forest).

At the end of the ninety-degree right fork are a couple of steps on a stone pedestal that terminates the path, or opens it up in the opposite direction. The opposite point leads to a platform higher up. After the temples the route crosses the stone bridge with the drainage pipe and leads through the two huge commemorative stones, which are tilted sideways and bear inscriptions. The complex would not have been designed by Bogdan Bogdanović if the abstract concept did not react to every feature of the landscape in such a way that one could just as well maintain that the design had emerged from the location.

The metamorphosis in the perception of the temples presents a theme of its own. From the distance, buildings placed peacefully in the landscape, rustic-looking with their gabled roofs and only conspicuous in their arrangement to one another (as a group of three).

8

The closer one comes, the more numerous and fuller, the more aggressive even, the relief of the closely rowed pillars appears. The surreal grimacing faces, called *monsters* by Bogdanović, could only be described by the architect to the clients, the building contractors and visitors as perhaps being an allusion to the banished grimaces of a future fascism looming (and how right he was). Apart from alluding to an uncanny world of the collective unconscious these stacked, condensed monstrous heads (*The Return of the Gryphon*, *The Horned Bird* etc., names used as book titles by B.B.) form a vast relief, as much in the Balkan light as in the

5, 7   diffused fog, of an unforgettable silhouette of doorways.

There is another interesting piece of information from B.B. himself: originally the temples were to have been adorned with only a few grimaces merely as acroteria. After this job the masons would have been unemployed and have had to return to their villages. They asked B.B. whether he would like to draw still more of these strange 'things'. So the job was extended by three years, and instead of about a dozen there are 620 of these headpieces (crockets). A remarkable social aspect of the planning process that would not have been possible in just any society (as can be read in *Der verdammte Baumeister*).

The complex at Čačak, which is peopled by pious strollers even on weekdays, represents a hardly imaginable contrast to the life of the city. Even though not walled in, there are no marked thresholds to be found to a sacred area; everybody notices the semantic hermeticism of the site on entering it. The untouched slope with a couple of implanted archaic reminders is transformed into a strangely atmospheric space for art, into a terrain of taut perception, of meditative reflection, not unlike gardens of the Far East which do not tend to beleaguer the mind but to inspire it.

2

3

4

5

6

7

8

124

Memorial Site with Mausoleum

for 4650 Fallen Partisans

Čačak, Serbia

126

Memorial Site with Mausoleum

for 4650 Fallen Partisans

Čačak, Serbia

(Bogdan Bogdanović, Peter Lachnit)

128

Memorial Site with Mausoleum

for 4650 Fallen Partisans

Čačak, Serbia

130
Memorial Site with Mausoleum
for 4650 Fallen Partisans
Čačak, Serbia

Bela Crkva
Serbia

Group of Cenotaphs

1971

Bela Crkva is considered to be where the first shot was fired at a collaborator with the occupying forces by insurgent Serbs. Locals today still report that, following a speech by a communist freedom fighter, when a country policeman enquired as to who had been speaking he was shot in the ensuing altercation.

This small but very impressive memorial site is a striking element integrated in the urban fabric of the town centre (opposite the bela crkva, the white church). It lies as a group of cenotaphs comprising nine figures between a former post office and a public house, and bears a strong similarity to the Mourning Women in Bihać, which also consist of five raw stone blocks piled up. Although the figures here are visibly male, which is to be seen alone by the suggestion of shakos (Šaikača hats). According to Ristić there had not been any plans of the complex, the positioning of the individual figures within the group had also clearly been established on location. Written on the small commemorative stone in front of the ensemble it says: *Here, Serbia cried 'freedom'*.

The spatial relationship of the memorial site to the church has a strong impact, emphasised by the distance of a pasture that lies in the landscape like a lake as an element of calm, of reflection and of mutual respect. The three stelae with busts in front of the former post office and the small monuments by the church are later components that try to establish a connection to Bogdanović's stylistic vocabulary.

A Flower for the Dead

1

2

3

4

134
Group of Cenotaphs
Bela Crkva, Serbia

136
Group of Cenotaphs
Bela Crkva, Serbia

Travnik
Bosnia and Herzegovina

Cenotaphs for the Victims of Fascism

1971–75

The memorial site is situated outside Travnik on the hill Smrike. It is an eerie place. It was a battle zone during the Bosnian War and there is apparently still a danger of unexploded landmines in the area. The twelve cenotaphs of porous bihacit sandstone looked like a group of *pairs of serpents* (Ristić) flocking together, each between 2.5 and 4.5 metres tall; seven of them still glare at visitors today with threatening and simultaneously frightened eyes.

2, 3

An overgrown, half-devastated location where a number of overgrown stones lie in the grass and scrub, alongside the remaining cenotaphs. Here one may be reminded of Bogomil tombstones, even if to a certain extent the similarity of the stones and the direction of their threatening gaze produce a cumulative collective effect. According to the Gnostics' creed the snakes could also be symbols of a positive world, one that ostracises its evil spirits. If one wishes to use the word 'magical' at all costs, then it would be apt for this place.

Note: This site, situated in Novi Travnik, can be reached via a country lane. Although it is not advisable to take this route as there might still be some landmines there. It is more advisable to walk a few hundred metres across private land from an inn on the highway.

Mass executions of Serb civilians by the Ustaše

A Flower for the Dead

1   2   3   4

140

Cenotaphs for the Victims of Fascism

Travnik, Bosnia and Herzegovina

142

Cenotaphs for the Victims of Fascism

Travnik, Bosnia and Herzegovina

Berane
Montenegro

Monument to Freedom

1972–77

The reafforestation of the surroundings of the remains of earthen fortifications from the Ottoman Empire with fir trees and other conifers on Jasikovac hill created a closed, deserted forest clearing which Bogdan Bogdanović has marked as a space with a freeform (approximately forty by sixty metres), almost closed ring of forty Herzegovinian gabbro stelae that follows the topography.

The stones are between 2.3 and 2.75 metres long, 1.3 and 1.45 metres tall and have an even thickness (depth) of 0.75 metres. They do not touch each other, either leaving a crack open or being slightly out of line at the ends. The result is not a wall but what looks like a wall that cannot be passed and which is also accentuated as a freestanding wreath by a twenty centimetre gap from the ground. The impression given is that of a hovering tyre or ring. An 18 metre tall cone clad with ornamented sandstone slabs forms an excentric focus on the southwesternmost edge of the ring and, although narrow, allows access from both sides to what is, to an extent, a protected space that makes the open-air room even more calmly introspective and more hermetic due to an arena-like slightly upwards slope to the floor (laid with stone slabs, but mixed with grass). The exterior of the stone ring is encircled by a broad strip of paved walkway. This heightens the place's significance as a concealed, conspiratorial meeting point and gathering place, later as a place of commemoration and celebration.

A characteristic feature of Bogdan Bogdanović's design process is the ambivalent meaning or function of the cone. On the one hand it is an archaic geometric shape of immense symbolic impact, extreme artificiality in contrast to the natural setting (the forest), but at the same time it is also in a formal dialogue with and closest approximation of the conifers' appearance. The earthen wall, partly gone and being reclaimed by nature, is to a certain extent also being artfully renewed, improved and, gaining in significance as an artefact and as a connection to history, brought to the fore visually.

The folkloric ornaments, quotations on the stelae from regional costume, and the Bogdanovićian calligraphic messages from three centuries of the extended family of Vasojević's local history pay tribute to Montenegrin culture. The inscriptions are historical messages, like: '*Around the middle of the seventeenth century there was an uprising among crop farmers in the Lim area, livestock farmers and serfs. The Ottomans devastated many villages.*' (Lim is a river.) There are also many inscriptions from more recent times: '27th March 1941 *Better the Grave than a Slave*', '3.10.1943, *Upper Polimlje. The Germans burned down*

1

the grammar school in Berane. The soldiers committed many atrocities', '*Brotherhood and Unity forged in battle*', or '*The local parliament in Berane has made the decision (21.7.1941) that the Yugoslavian tricolour is to be the flag to fly from the liberated zone.*'

As a result of its position in the countryside and its self-contained spatial structure, the complex is among the most atmospheric memorial sites by B.B. The fact that the lettering is difficult to read was taken by the building team and by the local population with humour. The tongue-in-cheek argument: In Berane 'every child knows the quotes off by heart', anyway. Or, perhaps more accurately: knew.

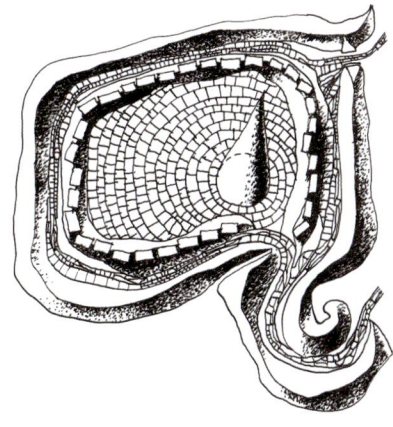

2

3

4

5

6

7

8

146
Monument to Freedom
Berane, Montenegro

148
Monument to Freedom
Berane, Montenegro

150

Monument to Freedom

Berane, Montenegro

152

Monument to Freedom

Berane, Montenegro

Vlasotince
Serbia

Shrine to the Fallen Freedom Fighters

1973–75

The small amphitheatre — not much larger than a country parlour — has a strange mixed ambience. With the familiar old photograph of Bogdan Bogdanović in mind the supposition is that the memorial site is to be found in a deserted spot on a mountain. In reality it is practically in the town and near by an agreeable inn, a day-tripper restaurant destination with a covered wooden terrace on the upper level. The memorial site lies next to it in a small wood on the edge of a cemetery on a ridge-top site with a view of the town and the valley of the river Vlasina. This view is blocked by a granite 'Guardian of the Revolution' (the client's term, according to Ristić) in the form of a tower fragment (a twelve metre tall pylon), whereby the amphitheatrical hollow lined by three rows of unconnected granite blocks is lent an unusual calm and intimacy in the wide open space. In addition, this archaic location, where talks, music, dance and even a camp fire are imaginable, is surrounded by blocks of granite weighing tonnes and described by Bogdanović as *stone flowers,* probably as an allusion to the decoration between *floral ornamentation and pictograms* that look like secret messages.

    The tower-like guardian, or the monumental stele, bears an enigmatic symbol in the centre — a rod split by a slit, with a blossom-like capital carrying a wheel that is half-open at the top. Furthermore, two paired discs are on the two edges of the tower that dissolve the borders of the volume rather than challenging them. Overall a quiet, peaceful place in a vicinity that is as silent as it is convivial.

1

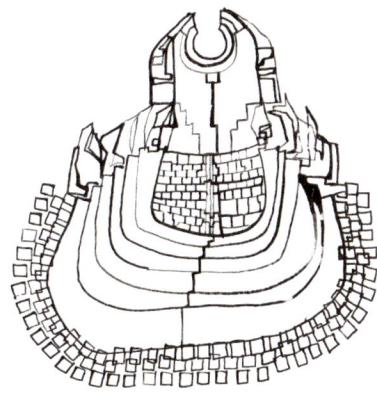

155

A Flower for the Dead

2 3 4 5 6 7 8

156

Shrine to the Fallen Freedom Fighters

Vlasotince, Serbia

158

Shrine to the Fallen Freedom Fighters

Vlasotince, Serbia

160

Shrine to the Fallen Freedom Fighters

Vlasotince, Serbia

Vukovar
Croatia

Dudik Memorial Park for the Victims of Fascism

1978 – 80

Even though the original terrain of the complex (a mulberry grove) is very cramped today by the advancing development, the memorial can still assert itself as an independent element of its own in the landscape of the urban periphery. The five 18 metre tall cones, now riddled with bullet holes and rising out of the ground like the tips of sunken towers, are encircled by a wall of raw diorite stones and crowned with points of copper sheeting (helmets). These are partly in tatters and have their impact today as ruins of hate and ignorance, making them the memorial for a memorial.

The sharp-tipped cones stand in a relationship with an existing group of trees. A flat, half-circular staircase (like a Greek arena) has been destroyed but is still discernible as a structure on the ground. The metaphorical image of a sunken or flooded town permits an association with water. From this the 27 small diorite ships with symmetrically curved gondola-like reliefs swimming, as if riding on waves, through the complex become comprehensible. The loose, or artificially random, grouping — according to Bogdanović, inspired by children moving freely in groups — creates a peculiarly cheerful hustle and bustle. Not to be over-looked: a number of massive mulberry bushes remind one of the place name, *dudik* = mulberry grove. So nature enters into a fascinating relationship with the spiritual space. After several rounds of the complex one's view sharpens for closer interspatial relationships. The apparently randomly floating little ships generate such relationships while marking positions.

The Water Tower

In actual fact the town's shot-up landmark has become the inadvertent memorial for a grim history. One cannot rob this testimonial to its time of its authenticity, to this extent too Bogdan Bogdanović's commemorative sites are historically endorsed, or first even more indelibly inscribed into the memory of the town by the traces of destruction. The baroque Vukovar was heavily damaged by the Serbian military as the 'hub of the Western world', and was scheduled for annexation and a Byzantine style rebuilding.

1

This is where the Ustaše shot members of the anti-fascist resistance and innocent civilians in 1941 and 1943. The memorial, also calling to mind a sunken town, has been lent an additional commemorative element by the ruins from the Croatian War of Independence (1991–1995).

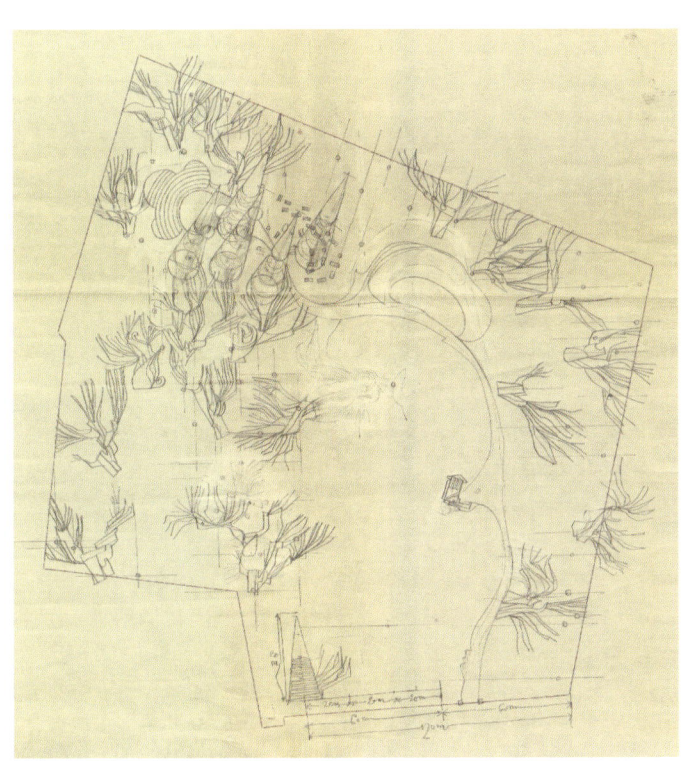

2

3

4

5

6

7

8

164

Dudik Memorial Park for the Victims of Fascism

Vukovar, Croatia

166

Dudik Memorial Park for the Victims of Fascism

Vukovar, Croatia

168

Dudik Memorial Park for the Victims of Fascism

Vukovar, Croatia

Popina near Trstenik
Serbia

Combatants' Mausoleum

1979–81

The mausoleum is among the last and probably one of the most impressive and stringent of Bogdan Bogdanović's works. It lies on Nebrak, a hill, above the small river Popina with an open view into the valley where the first major battle took place between Tito's Partisans and the German occupying forces, with 42 dead. The gentle slope faces northeast.

The monument develops in a line along a viewing axis of sixty metres in length consisting of four components and three intervals. The starting point is a modest stone cube. The second element, forty paces away, consists of three thick, arch-shaped monolithic granite slabs, one set closely behind the other, each with a large circular opening of about three metres in diameter. The third element (twenty paces away) is a towering triangle about 18 metres in height and ten paces deep, with a circular opening about five metres in diameter. The last element is (at a distance of 13 paces) a single arch-shaped slab with the same moon or sun gateway.

One could also describe the way the elements line up in a poetic rhyme scheme: *a b c b* or, even more accurately: *a bbb c b*, which generates enormous dynamism (acceleration) on the one hand, while at the end *b c b* uses mirror imagery, inversion or symmetry consolidated into a static constellation. The line of sight is caught in the distance by a forested hillside; it ends in a no longer clearly perceptible, distant world. The visitor pauses in the last spatial sequence (in front of the moon gateway), looks into the distance or back, sees self-reflexive lines of lettering and persists in looking, at once irritated and fascinated. The words — *If need be, repeat me* — are the result of a competition for schoolchildren and underline the metaphorical quality of the location, giving it a striking temporal dimension. One finds oneself in a spatial constellation thread along an axis, detached from all reality, in an irrational space, even in a space-accelerator of magical intensity. One is preoccupied with a kind of imaginary ray of light in a true infinitude. The place remains this-worldly, however, more reminiscent of an archaic calendar structure, the dialogue with a cosmic world is encapsulated in a concrete poetic configuration.

For whatever reason, all of the surreal reliefs and ornamentation have gone from this mausoleum, only the calligraphic inscriptions evoke the author's long-held partiality for the ancient. In their visually exuberant opulence Bogdan Bogdanović's necropolises frequently border on a glossolalia of symbols, while the Popina mausoleum concentrates impressively on geometric elements and their related sculptural manifestations. The square, the triangle and the circle, inexhaustible because not clearly definable symbols of mankind's structuring

and searching, are captivatingly placed in the landscape as built verse. The fascination lies, however, not so much in the elemental and in the dimensions of the complex but in its poetic idiom, in the lines, repetition and rhythm of the elements. Here Bogdan Bogdanović shows himself to be a true poet, one who knows that a precise statement is not merely the product of words (vocabulary) but of the interrelationships, the constellations, which transform the site into an unforgettable place, one that entrenches itself indelibly in the memory and remains a place of remembrance irrespective of historical specifics.

Here, too, the mausoleum, as it is called, is a self-defining area in the landscape that does not de facto fence itself off. The pyramid is visible almost incidentally through the bushes, if it has not already been spotted from the highway. And one leaves again without any staging of the departure. The axis, though, which connects the stone monuments, the imaginary tunnel where the gaze develops the intensity of a laser, sticks in the mind as the magical element of the place.

Postscript: On a second visit we found the conventional approach from the road (we came from a small wood behind the monument with Bogdanović in 2003). Although the approach to the monument from behind is more attractive because it unfolds starting from the cube with an inscription. Coming from the road one arrives at the head, grabbing, so to speak, the bull by the horns. The complex is probably the most individual and the least playful, a complex that does not conceal its roots in French revolutionary architecture. I have attempted to figure out the distances (the rhythmic sequence) with paces. Unfortunately the complex has been disfigured by brutal tyre tracks and earthworks. It is clearly used for motocross racing and the like.

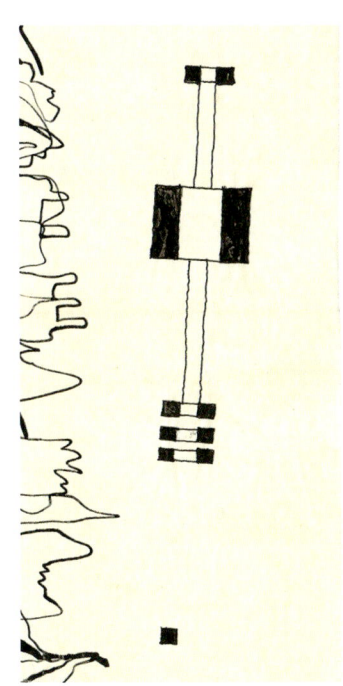

2

3

4

5

6

7

8

172

Combatants' Mausoleum

Popina near Trstenik, Serbia

174
Combatants' Mausoleum
Popina near Trstenik, Serbia

175

176
Combatants' Mausoleum
Popina near Trstenik, Serbia

178

Combatants' Mausoleum

Popina near Trstenik, Serbia

Translation: *If need be, repeat me.*

Afterword and Acknowledgements

As important as documents, eye-witnesses, reports etc. are for a memorial, it is essential to have viewed the sites themselves first-hand. This is particularly true of Bogdan Bogdanović's complexes, which, as spatial concepts and elements of a topography and the surrounding landscape, demand this direct experience. It cannot be substituted by drawings, plans and photographs.

The impressions conveyed in this book are indebted to numerous trips to the sites which I could never have undertaken alone, and to friendly aids; most of the information is owed to conversations with Bogdan and Ksenija Bogdanović as well as the books by B.B. that have been translated into German.

The most impressive prelude came in August 2002 on the occasion of B.B.'s eightieth birthday, when Peter Lachnit took me to Belgrade with him while doing research for the ORF [the Austrian Broadcasting Corporation]. We were fortunate enough, apart from being given an extensive tour of the city, not only to visit the memorial site in the Jewish cemetery in Belgrade with the still sprightly B.B., but also the sites in Čačak, Kruševac and Popina — covering the full array, from his first to his last work.

On the subsequent trip from Zagreb to Jasenovac in September 2004, we were the guests of Nataša Jovičić, the director of the Memorial Museum, with whom, alongside an extensive tour, we also received a very informative insight into the comprehensive collection of documentation.

The third, far more extensive and exhaustive trip was undertaken in May 2009 with a group working on the major B.B. exhibition held at the Architekturzentrum Wien, supervised by the exhibition's curator Ivan Ristić. We visited almost all of the sites on this tour — excluding only those of Bela Crkva, Berane and Kosovska Mitrovica. The roughly 4,000 kilometres covered on this trip also provided us with wonderful impressions of the culture and countryside of former Yugoslavia.

In September 2011 my wife and I travelled to Berane in Montenegro to fill the gap. The Austrian embassy there was very helpful, putting us in touch with the Berane community and Monika Stanic-Orovic, who gave us a guided tour and a subsequent translation of the inscriptions on the monoliths.

In July 2012 we succeeded in travelling (accompanied by Gisela and Boris Podrecca) to Kosovska Mitrovica, which had not been possible on a first attempt from Pristina (with the intervention of the former Vice-Chancellor of Austria Erhard Busek via KFOR) because the site lies in the Serbian part of Kosovska Mitrovica. Thanks to an introduction by Prof. Vladimir Vuković to the architect Ljubiša Folić (professor at the University of Technology in Kosovska Mitrovica) and his great hospitality and numerous tours of the memorial site and to monasteries in both parts of the region, we finally received key information locally.

A return trip to Bihać and Mostar (Bosnia and Herzegovina) was undertaken in October 2012 with the invaluable assistance of the graphic designer of this book Gabriele Lenz and the architect Ulrich Huhs, when I was able to take photographs under better lighting conditions.

The last trip to Bela Crkva, in March 2013, took place thanks to Vladimir Vuković, who put us in touch with Vesna Vučinić (Vienna/Belgrade) who, in turn, used her extensive knowledge and savvy to get us from Belgrade to Bela Crkva. This was in connection with an informative conversation with the former assistant and student of B.B.'s Prof. Dimitrije Mladenović, which was the fruitful conclusion to all the research.

My very special thanks to my friends Ingrid and Christian Reder and to ERSTE Foundation for their generous promise of support, and without whose help this book could not have been completed. Finally, I should like to thank the publishers, the publishing director Herbert Ohrlinger and his staff for their highly committed collaboration, and not least Gabriele Lenz and Elena Henrich for the exemplary design of this book, and Jonathan Quinn for the conscientious translation.

Bibliography

Bogdan Bogdanović:

Die Stadt und der Tod, Wieser Verlag, Klagenfurt 1993

Architektur der Erinnerung, Wieser Verlag, Klagenfurt 1994

Die Stadt und die Zukunft, Wieser Verlag, Klagenfurt 1997

Der verdammte Baumeister, Paul Zsolnay Verlag Wien, Vienna 1997

Vom Glück in den Städten, Paul Zsolnay Verlag Wien, Vienna 2002

Die grüne Schachtel, Paul Zsolnay Verlag Wien, Vienna 2007

Ivan Ristić:

Bogdan Bogdanović — Baumeister und Zeichner (dissertation), 2010

Vladimir Vukovic:

Das literarische Werk des Architekten Bogdan Bogdanović, Anfänge, Entwicklung und das Thema Stadt, Verlag Anton Pustet, Salzburg 2009

Architekturzentrum Wien:

Bogdan Bogdanović, Memoria und Utopie in Tito-Jugoslawien (exhibition catalogue with essays by Ivan Ristić, Ursa Komac and Pablo Guillén, Heike Karge, Dragana Milovanovic, Vladimir Vukovic and Friedrich Achleitner), Wieser Verlag, Klagenfurt 2009